This book is for my parents,
who encouraged me to explore
and question everything and
have regretted it ever since.

B.R.

LADYBIRD BOOKS

UK | USA | Canada | Ireland | Australia
India | New Zealand | South Africa

Ladybird Books is part of the Penguin Random House group of companies
whose addresses can be found at global.penguinrandomhouse.com.

www.penguin.co.uk   www.puffin.co.uk   www.ladybird.co.uk

First published 2019
This paperback edition 2020
001

Printed in Latvia
A CIP catalogue record for this book is available from the British Library
ISBN: 978–0–241–36101–6

All correspondence to:
Ladybird Books, Penguin Random House Children's
80 Strand, London WC2R 0RL

Hidden Planet

BEN ROTHERY

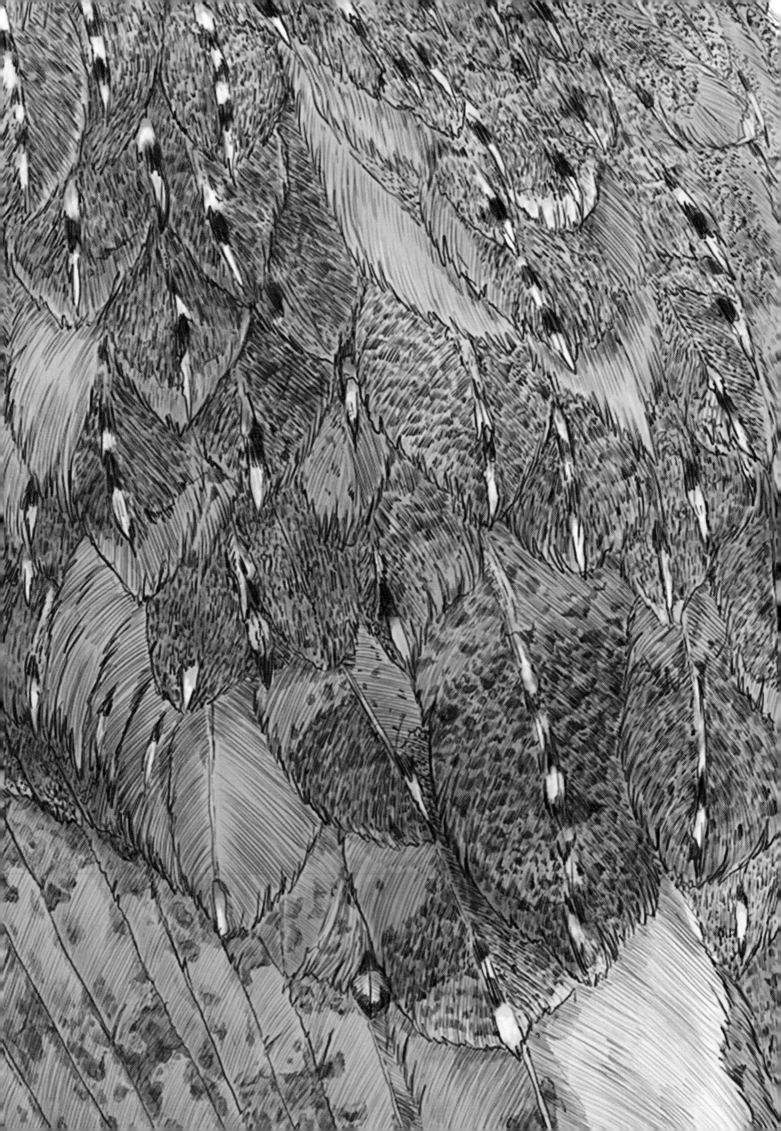

Contents

INTRODUCTION

I've always described myself as a frustrated naturalist trapped in an illustrator's body. I grew up wanting to be a mixture of TV presenter David Attenborough and fictional adventurer Indiana Jones, and eventually settled on illustration as a way of bringing my childhood fantasies to life. Now, I explore the natural world through drawing and writing – but it's not enough for me to produce a technically accurate picture of an animal. I also need to understand what's happening beneath the fur and the feathers.

I spent my early years travelling back and forth between the United Kingdom and southern Africa. I learned to swim in a mountain river, and one of my earliest memories is of being driven across the endless red dunes of the Namib Desert on my sixth birthday. As a child, I was never without an encyclopedia. When I wasn't reading about animals or drawing them, I was marvelling at anything I could find – from chameleons to crickets, and everything in between – and trying to understand it all.

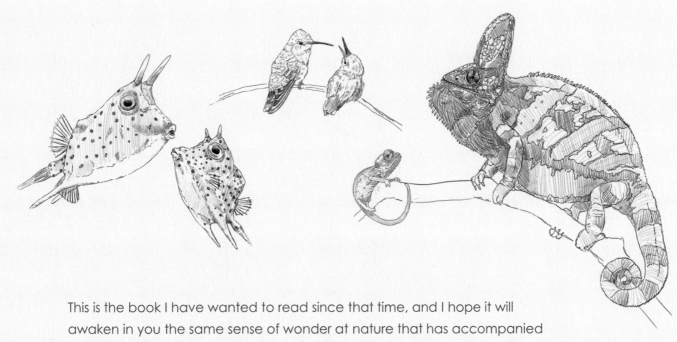

This is the book I have wanted to read since that time, and I hope it will awaken in you the same sense of wonder at nature that has accompanied me throughout my life. This book is my love letter to Planet Earth. It is a celebration of her hidden species, from the bold and beautiful to the interesting but ugly. It is the story of my favourite birds and animals; some are endangered, and others less so. It isn't a complete list but it will, I hope, offer a glimpse of the outstanding diversity of nature, as told from the perspective of a wildlife-obsessed boy and the detail-obsessed illustrator he became.

Ben Rothery

Aged 6 and 33

Spotted eagle owl
Bubo africanus

INTRODUCTION

I've always described myself as a frustrated naturalist trapped in an illustrator's body. I grew up wanting to be a mixture of TV presenter David Attenborough and fictional adventurer Indiana Jones, and eventually settled on illustration as a way of bringing my childhood fantasies to life. Now, I explore the natural world through drawing and writing – but it's not enough for me to produce a technically accurate picture of an animal. I also need to understand what's happening beneath the fur and the feathers.

I spent my early years travelling back and forth between the United Kingdom and southern Africa. I learned to swim in a mountain river, and one of my earliest memories is of being driven across the endless red dunes of the Namib Desert on my sixth birthday. As a child, I was never without an encyclopedia. When I wasn't reading about animals or drawing them, I was marvelling at anything I could find – from chameleons to crickets, and everything in between – and trying to understand it all.

Contents

HIDDEN PLANET

When we think of something as being hidden, we normally imagine a creature that is out of sight or cleverly disguised as something else. Perhaps it is cunning, shy or sly. Maybe it is small or comes out only under the cover of darkness. It may live deep in a rainforest or in a cave, bury itself in the sand or spend its life high in the treetops.

There are also hidden relationships between species that might seem otherwise unconnected. For many years, humans have invented fantastical stories to explain these connections. One more secret of Planet Earth can be found in the unexpected abilities and behaviours of some of the creatures we think we already know.

The creatures in this book are hidden in some or all of these ways.

Hidden relationships

One example of the sometimes hidden relationships between different species is symbiosis, which is when two or more organisms live closely together. There are three main kinds of symbiotic relationship: commensalism, mutualism and parasitism. Each of these relationships has multiple versions with different characteristics, but all require a certain amount of balance between the species involved.

Commensalism

In a commensal relationship, one organism benefits while the other is neither harmed nor helped. Many bird species, such as the southern carmine bee-eater, for example, perch on the backs of elephants and other large animals, feeding on the insects disturbed by the bigger creatures' movements.

Southern carmine bee-eater
Merops nubicoides

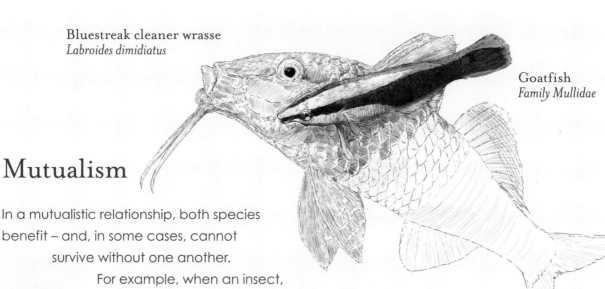

Bluestreak cleaner wrasse
Labroides dimidiatus

Goatfish
Family Mullidae

Mutualism

In a mutualistic relationship, both species benefit – and, in some cases, cannot survive without one another. For example, when an insect, bird or bat feeds on nectar from a flower, then visits other flowers of the same species, both the plant and the creature benefit. The animal gets an energy-rich meal in the form of the nectar and in turn carries pollen to the next plant, which helps the plant to reproduce. Some birds and fish feed on the parasites that infest the skin of larger animals. Oxpeckers, for example, feed on the parasites on oxen, and cleaner wrasse on grouper fish. In different circumstances, the bigger animal might have made a meal of the small bird or fish, but instead both species benefit: the smaller one gets a meal, while the larger is kept free of irritating pests.

Bumblebee
Genus Bombus

Parasitism

In a parasitic relationship one organism – the parasite – benefits at the expense of the other – the host. Perhaps the parasite feeds on the host's blood, like a vampire bat or mosquito does, or it gets the unwitting host to raise its babies either alongside or instead of the host's own, like some birds, fish and insects do. However, even a parasitic relationship requires a great deal of balance, as the parasite needs the host to live long enough for the parasite to accomplish its goal.

Mosquito
Family Culicidae

Mutualism

Common clownfish (Amphiprion ocellaris)

The instantly recognizable common clownfish is a small orange, white and black fish that grows up to 11 centimetres long. Like many other fish species, the female clownfish is a lot larger than the male. They live in groups with one dominant female and one smaller male breeding, while the others care for the nest and defend their home.

The clownfish is the perfect example of a mutualistic relationship. There are around 30 species of clownfish, and they all form relationships with sea anemones, with both life forms providing a number of benefits to the other. The clownfish keep the anemones free of parasites and defend them from predators, such as angelfish. The constant movement of the little fish in and out of an anemone's tentacles increases water flow, which brings in food and helps keep the anemone clean. The anemone even absorbs nutrients from the clownfish's excrement, helping it to grow larger.

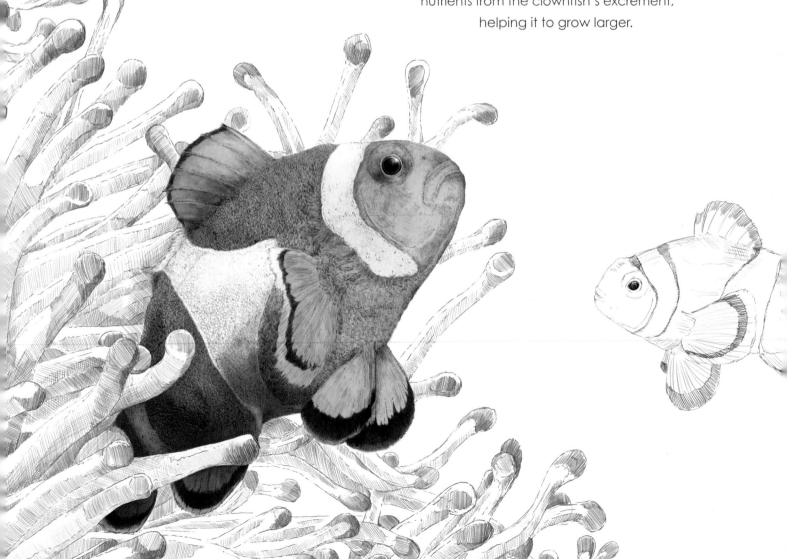

In turn, the anemone provides the clownfish with a home and a nursery for their babies, and protects them from predators with its stinging tentacles. The anemone also supplies food in the form of leftover scraps from its meals, parasites and the occasional discarded tentacle.

Sea anemones are poisonous and feed on fish, stinging them with their tentacles before consuming them, so clownfish have developed a hidden way to survive this mutualistic relationship through evolution, which is the way that types of living things change over time. A clownfish's body is coated in special mucus that prevents the anemone from recognizing it as food, meaning it doesn't get stung.

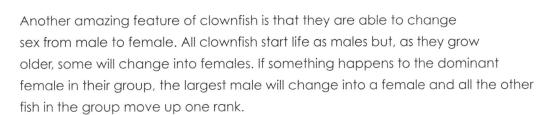

Another amazing feature of clownfish is that they are able to change sex from male to female. All clownfish start life as males but, as they grow older, some will change into females. If something happens to the dominant female in their group, the largest male will change into a female and all the other fish in the group move up one rank.

Common clownfish are found near the coasts of Southeast Asia, Japan and northern Australia, but, despite their name, they are becoming threatened due to their popularity as an aquarium fish.

Reed warbler
Acrocephalus scirpaceus

Parasitism

Common cuckoo (Cuculus canorus)

The common cuckoo is a little bird with a big secret. Despite its innocent appearance, pretty feathers and lilting 'cuc-koo' call, the cuckoo is a parasite. Cuckoos engage in 'brood parasitism', which is where one species relies on another to raise its young. Doing this frees up time for the parasite species to look for food and produce more offspring. The cuckoo tricks other birds, such as warblers, wagtails and robins, into raising its chicks through a number of clever strategies based around 'mimicry', or imitating features of the other birds.

Adult cuckoos mimic certain birds of prey, including the Eurasian sparrowhawk, a predatory bird that preys primarily on other birds. Since the cuckoo is roughly the same size as the sparrowhawk and has an almost identical barred pattern on the feathers of its underside, many small birds are frightened of it. They will flee when the cuckoo approaches their nest, rather than defend it. This clever mimicry allows the cuckoo to frighten the other bird away for long enough to land in the nest, push out one of the eggs already there and lay its own egg, before making its escape. The whole process takes only about ten seconds.

14

Common cuckoo
Cuculus canorus

Once the cuckoo has laid its egg, the second
strategy takes over. Cuckoos employ 'egg mimicry',
which means they lay eggs that resemble those of the
host species. So, for example, female cuckoos that target
reed warblers will stick to this species and lay eggs that, while larger,
have a similar pattern and colour to the warbler's.

The host species will unwittingly incubate the cuckoo's egg alongside its own.
The cuckoo's egg often hatches earlier than the other chicks, and this is when the
third – and nastiest – strategy comes into play. The newly hatched cuckoo chick
will wait until the parent bird is out gathering food, then it will push the other eggs
out of the nest so that it gets all the care and attention of its new parents.

During the spring and summer, when they breed, common cuckoos can be
found all across Europe and much of Asia. In the autumn, they migrate to Africa
to spend the winter there.

A Pacific hermit crab (*Coenobita compressus*) using a discarded bottle top as protection

Hermit crabs

There are approximately 1,100 species of hermit crab worldwide, and they share a fascinating connection with sea snails and some other shellfish. Hermit crabs have no shells of their own, so they use the other creatures' discarded shells to protect their soft and vulnerable bodies. While this connection is not part of a symbiotic relationship because the shells are not alive, the way a hermit crab selects and uses its adopted shell is remarkable nevertheless.

Hermit crabs vary massively in size, from less than a centimetre to almost a metre. The giant coconut crab, which can grow up to a metre in length, also lives for over 60 years. They are actually more closely related to squat lobsters and crayfish than they are to true crabs.

Only the front part of a hermit crab's body is hard, which is why it uses an empty shell or another salvaged item for protection. Most species of hermit crab have bodies that curve round in a spiral to better fit inside and grip on to their adopted homes. When threatened, a hermit crab will fully retract into the shell and seal the entrance with its claws.

As hermit crabs grow, they need larger and larger shells, but these can be hard to find. If they can't find a properly sized shell, they will sometimes resort to wearing other items, including rubbish. This has become increasingly common, in part because of a decrease in the number of available shells due to humans collecting them, but also because of the amount of plastic and other debris in the ocean.

This scarcity of shells has led to the development of some interesting behaviour. Hermit crabs will sometimes form 'vacancy chains' in order to exchange shells with one another. When a hermit crab finds an empty shell, it will leave its own to inspect the new one. If the shell fits, the crab will abandon its old home and move in to the new one; if the shell doesn't fit, however, the crab will do something quite incredible. The crab returns to its old shell and proceeds to wait – sometimes for up to eight hours – for other crabs to come along. When a newcomer arrives, it inspects the shell, and if it also finds the shell too large it will return to its own shell and wait. In this way, a group of up to 20 waiting crabs can form, with each crab holding on to the next crab in line, from the largest to the smallest. Eventually, a crab arrives that is the perfect fit for the empty shell. It moves in to its new home, leaving its old shell empty, and the waiting crabs quickly swap shells in sequence, each moving up in size.

Hermit crabs in a vacancy chain

Brown bear
Ursus arctos

HIDDEN FAMILIES

West Indian manatee
Trichechus manatus

Cape fur seal
Arctocephalus pusillus

Among the most fascinating things on Planet Earth are the strange, hidden and unexpected family relationships that exist between seemingly unconnected animals.

Who would think, to look at them, that the elephant's closest relatives are the manatee, the dugong and the rock hyrax? Or that the rhinoceros is related to the tapir? And would you believe that the hippo is related to the dolphin? Or that seals, sea lions and walruses are not related to whales, dolphins or manatees, but rather to bears and weasels?

Let's take a look at some of nature's more unusual families, and the hidden things that connect them.

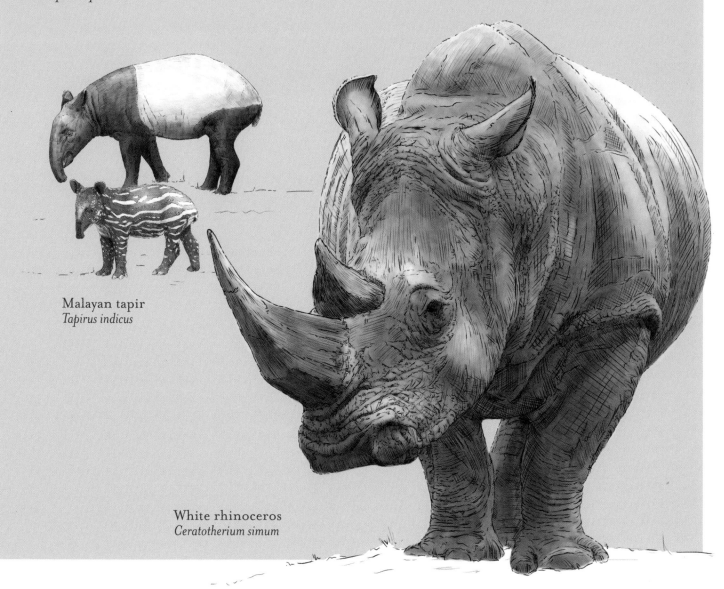

Malayan tapir
Tapirus indicus

White rhinoceros
Ceratotherium simum

Rock hyrax
Procavia capensis

A hyrax is a small, fat, furry plant-eating mammal with a permanently suspicious expression and some highly unexpected cousins. Despite being roughly the size of a large rabbit, the hyrax's closest relatives are the elephant and the manatee, with whom they share a common ancestor. There are five species of hyrax: the rock hyrax, the yellow spotted rock hyrax, and the western, eastern and southern tree hyraxes. It is the rock hyrax that most interests me.

I first encountered rock hyraxes, which are known in South Africa as dassies, on family trips to Cape Town. I immediately fell in love with them. As I watched this funny buck-toothed little animal with stubby legs scurry from rock to rock on the slopes of Table Mountain, I could only marvel at how it was able to scramble up the sheer rocks with an agility quite out of keeping with its appearance – but then I suppose you'd do the same if snakes and eagles were trying to eat you!

The key to the rock hyrax's astonishing climbing ability lies in its sweaty feet. The soles of a hyrax's feet are covered with large, soft pads that are kept moist by special secretions, which allow them to literally stick to the rocks.

African bush elephant
Loxodonta africana

Rock hyraxes are social creatures, living in
groups of anywhere from 10 to 80 individuals.
They forage for food as a group, with one standing watch – usually the
dominant male – while the others graze on a wide variety of plants, including
some that are toxic to other animals.

Rock hyraxes are lazy creatures, and spend up to 95 per cent
of their time resting. This is due, in part, to their inability to
fully control their internal temperature. Like reptiles,
hyraxes need to lie in the sun to capture heat in the
mornings and evenings, and cannot go out in the
hotter parts of the day for fear of overheating.

Although hyraxes are still common throughout Africa
and parts of the Middle East, they are increasingly
vulnerable to habitat changes. As humans build ever
more settlements and roads, it becomes harder for
hyraxes to relocate and to find food, shelter and
mates. Hyraxes and many other animals
find themselves isolated on hills and
mountains, like little islands
adrift in a sea of
towns and cities.

Okapi

Okapia johnstoni

The okapi is a large plant-eating mammal whose closest living relative – despite the fact it looks more like a zebra – is the giraffe. This shy, solitary animal is native to the Democratic Republic of the Congo, where it lives in forests at an altitude of 500 to 1,500 metres above sea level.

Cape giraffe
Giraffa camelopardalis giraffa

Their partially striped pattern and dark, chestnut-coloured fur are perfect camouflage, allowing them to blend in seamlessly with the trees and fragmented sunlight that filters down into their dense rainforest home. Even though they're large and mostly active during the day, okapis were completely unknown to the Western world until the beginning of the twentieth century.

Okapi
Okapia johnstoni

Despite the big difference in size and neck length between okapis and their closest living relative, the giraffe, both animals have exactly the same number of vertebrae in their necks: seven

Okapis have huge tongues that can be up to 45 centimetres long. Their tongues are 'prehensile', which means an okapi can use its tongue to grab and pull on the leaves, grasses, fruits and fungi that make up its diet – much like how an elephant uses its trunk. Some of the plants okapis eat are known to be toxic, and it has been suggested that the reason they eat clay and sometimes even the charcoal from burned forest trees is to balance the effects of the poisonous leaves and fruit in their diet.

Due to their secretive nature and to their remote and inhospitable habitat, which is difficult for most humans to travel in, okapis are hard to observe in the wild. As a result, there are only estimates of their population, and there are thought to be just 25,000 left. This classifies the okapi as endangered.

Common ostrich
Struthio camelus

Ratites

The ratites are a diverse group of five different species of birds found throughout the southern hemisphere. The ostrich is found in Africa, the rhea in South America and Germany, the emu in Australia, the cassowary in Australia, Indonesia and Papua New Guinea, and the kiwi – the runt of the litter – in New Zealand.

Most are large, some have dagger-sharp talons, snakelike necks or fluffy feathers, and they all hide a secret in their wings: the ratites cannot fly.

The ostrich, the largest of the ratites, stands up to 3 metres tall, can weigh over 150 kilograms and runs at speeds of up to 44 miles per hour. That's faster than a racehorse, which makes sense given that ostriches share the African continent with lions, leopards, cheetahs, hyenas and wild dogs – all of which would like to eat them!

At just under 2 metres tall, the emu is the second-largest ratite, with the cassowary coming in third at 1.5 metres. The rhea is just over a metre tall, while the little kiwi stands at around 45 centimetres in height – no larger than a chicken. Each of these amazing flightless birds is supremely adapted for life on the ground.

For all but the kiwi, long legs and great stamina allow them to walk huge distances in search of food and water, and to run at great speeds if necessary. The cassowary, with its powerful legs and dagger-like claws, is also a capable and aggressive fighter that will defend its territory and nest to the death if challenged.

The kiwi leads an altogether different life from the other ratites. As the only nocturnal member of the ratite group, which means they are mostly active at night, the challenges kiwis face have given rise to some interesting adaptations. Kiwis are almost blind – in fact, relative to their size, they have the smallest eye of any bird. This means that they rely heavily on their other senses – particularly smell – to find the insects, worms and small amphibians that make up most of their diet. A kiwi's bill is long, bendy and sensitive, making it perfect for probing in the soil for food. Uniquely among birds, the kiwi's nostrils are located at the tip of its beak rather than close to its face. As a result, the kiwi can locate its food underground without seeing or even feeling it.

Despite their adaptations, and the fact that they have been around since the end of the time of their extinct dinosaur relatives, all five species of ratite are under threat. This is caused by a mixture of habitat loss, hunting and other human impact, so they will need our help to survive.

Common ostrich chick
Struthio camelus

Emu
Dromaius novaehollandiae

It is the male emu who incubates the eggs. Once his mate has laid the clutch, he will neither eat nor drink until the eggs hatch, and in fact will only stand up to turn his eggs, which he does about ten times a day. Over the eight weeks that he cares for the eggs, he will lose up to one third of his total body weight.

Southern cassowary
Casuarius casuarius

Cassowaries have three-toed feet with very sharp claws. Their second toe in particular sports a dagger-like claw that can be up to 12.5 centimetres long. A cassowary uses this claw as a weapon to defend its territory from rivals, and it protects its nest from predators by kicking out with its powerful legs.

Greater rhea
Rhea americana

Although all three species of rhea are native to South America, there is also a small population living in Germany. In late 2000, seven birds – three males and four females – escaped near the town of Lübeck and, despite efforts to capture them, they remained free. Now, there are nearly 150 rhea living happily on the floodplains of the river Wakenitz.

Common ostrich
Struthio camelus

Although the ostrich's egg is the largest of any bird species, it is actually the smallest relative to the bird's body size. The popular belief that ostriches bury their heads in the sand when threatened, because they think that doing so makes them invisible, has been around since Roman times, but it's not true. In fact, the ostrich sticks its head into the sand to swallow sand and stones in order to help it digest the chewy plants and seeds it eats.

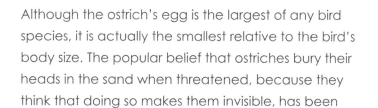

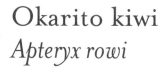

Okarito kiwi
Apteryx rowi

Unlike the other ratites, which nest on the ground, the kiwi lays its eggs in burrows, and its short legs and stocky body are ideally suited to this. Unlike the ostrich, the kiwi lays eggs that are enormous relative to its body size. In fact, a kiwi's egg is six times larger than a chicken's, even though the birds are roughly the same size.

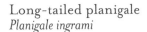

Long-tailed planigale
Planigale ingrami

Marsupials

Marsupials are a group of mammals found mostly in Australasia –
the range of islands in the South Pacific that includes Australia,
New Zealand, New Guinea, and other neighbouring islands. Nearly
70 per cent of the 334 species are found in Australasia alone, with
the remainder in South and Central America. Marsupials vary greatly
in size, from the Australian red kangaroo – which can stand up to
2.1 metres tall and jump up to 9 metres in a single bound – to the
tiny long-tailed planigale – not only the smallest marsupial, but
one of the smallest of all mammal species, with a body length
of around 6 centimetres.

Red kangaroo
Macropus rufus

Koala
Phascolarctos cinereus

Marsupials are hairy and their young feed on milk. As a result of this, the differences between marsupials and other types of mammals are not obvious. However, marsupials differ from other mammals in a number of fascinating ways. The most striking of these is the manner in which they raise their young. Most mammalian species are 'placental mammals', which means that, when pregnant, the mother grows a special organ called a placenta to feed her growing baby while it is still inside her body. This means that, for many species, the baby is already quite developed by the time it is born, and this is particularly common among large plant-eating mammals – baby antelopes, giraffes and elephants, for example, are able to walk and run only a few hours after being born.

Marsupials, on the other hand, take an entirely different approach. Their young are born small and under-developed, usually blind and totally hairless. A newborn marsupial has to crawl through its mother's fur to a special pouch where it lives and develops until it is large enough to fend for itself. The name marsupial even comes from this behaviour, as the pouch is known as a 'marsupium'.

Common wombat
Vombatus ursinus

For over 100 million years, many marsupials have evolved in geographical isolation from other animal species. In that time, they have developed not only many of their weird and wonderful abilities, but also filled the roles occupied by other mammals in different locations. Groups of kangaroos (known as 'mobs') move across the land like deer, grazing on plants; tiny planigales scurry through the leaf litter like mice; and sugar gliders soar from tree to tree in search of fruit and sweet sap, using a special flap of skin to glide, much like flying squirrels do.

Marsupials have even evolved to fill the space occupied elsewhere by moles. There are two species of marsupial mole, which spend their lives underground searching for beetle larvae. So well adapted are they for a life tunnelling that their pouches even face backwards so they don't fill with soil as the animal digs.

Peacock mantis shrimp
Odontodactylus scyllarus

HIDDEN ABILITIES

One of the things I love about animals is that there is often more to them than meets the eye – even the ones we think we know.

Some creatures have incredible abilities that aren't immediately obvious based on their appearance. The mantis shrimp – a relative of crabs and lobsters that's named after the land-dwelling praying mantis – might be small, but it's also very strong and aggressive for its size. It preys upon other small sea creatures, and cripples them with one of the fastest punches in nature, striking them incredibly hard with a pair of hinged arms usually kept folded away under its head. It launches these arms faster than a bullet from a rifle – so fast, in fact, that the movement causes the water in front of the punching arms to boil. As the water rapidly boils, it creates bubbles, which quickly pop and release energy. This process is called cavitation, and it is both this and the force of the mantis shrimp's punch that help it smash even the thickest of shells.

Meanwhile, we might think that we can see everything there is to know about other species, but under an animal's fur or feathers can lie all manner of hidden things. You wouldn't necessarily think that a beetle's hard shell is actually protection for a delicate pair of wings, or that a woodpecker's tongue is wrapped all the way round the inside of its skull. You wouldn't know just by looking at amphibians like frogs, newts and salamanders that they can breathe through their skin as well as their mouths, which allows them to stay underwater for longer.

Stag beetle
Lucanus cervus

Other times, we wrongly identify parts of a creature when the real part is hidden or not what we expect. For example, a flamingo's long legs might appear to bend backwards at the knee, but this is not the case. Flamingos actually stand on their tiptoes, meaning that what we think is their knee is actually their ankle, while their knee is located close to their body and hidden by feathers.

The creatures in this section all have abilities that don't seem obvious to us at first glance.

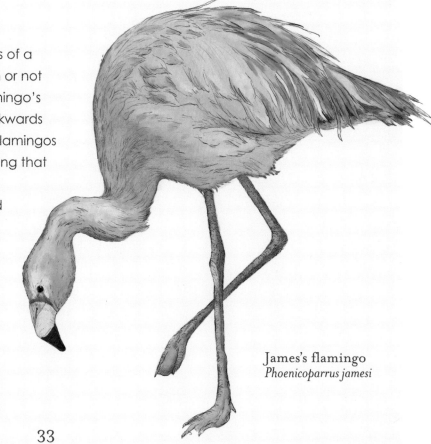

James's flamingo
Phoenicoparrus jamesi

Octopuses

It would be hard to find a better example of a creature with hidden abilities than the octopus. These strange eight-limbed molluscs are capable of extraordinary things, including solving complex problems and changing colour and shape – even large octopuses can squeeze through holes the size of a coin.

These incredible creatures are found in many parts of the world, and vary massively in size. The tiny star-sucker pygmy octopus (*Octopus wolfi*) measures less than 2.5 centimetres long, and weighs less than a gram, while the giant Pacific octopus (*Enteroctopus dofleini*) can measure almost 5 metres long.

The undersides of an octopus's limbs are covered with circular, adhesive suckers that allow the octopus to anchor itself, to move objects and to grab hold of its prey, which it then passes towards the beaklike mouthparts situated underneath its body.

Octopuses are highly intelligent. Not only do they have a large central brain, but each of their eight limbs also contains its own 'mini brain'. This enables an octopus to complete tasks with its limbs more quickly and effectively than other species, as each limb is able to act independently – moving, touching and even tasting – without direction from the central brain.

Octopuses are also masters of disguise. They have thousands of specialized cells called chromatophores hidden under their skin, which help them to change colour in an instant and to mimic the colour of objects and organisms around them. In addition, they also have small areas of skin called papillae, which they can expand or contract rapidly. An octopus uses these papillae to change both the shape and texture of its body, so that it can appear like anything from seaweed and rocks to another species altogether.

If its disguise fails, an octopus has more tricks up its eight sleeves.

When threatened, an octopus is able to squirt a thick cloud of
ink into the face of a would-be attacker. Also, it can
then quickly jet off and away by forcing water
through its siphon, an organ which
it also uses to breathe.

Common octopus
Octopus vulgaris

African leopard
Panthera pardus pardus

CAMOUFLAGE

An animal uses camouflage to make itself hard to see or to disguise itself as something else. Many species camouflage themselves to hide from predators or to help them catch their prey – and some do it for both reasons, hunting and hiding in a seemingly endless game of hide-and-seek, using shape, colour, texture and tactics to trick the eye and blend in to the environment.

When camouflaged for a particular habitat, a species may be plain in order to blend in with a particular colour, like a polar bear against snow and ice, or it may be coloured and patterned to look like its surroundings. Potoos are birds from South America with brownish patterned feathers that blend in with their environment by perching on trees so that they look like inedible broken stumps or branches.

Another way for an animal to hide in its surroundings is by using patterns, such as spots or stripes, to break up its outline and help it blend in to the background.

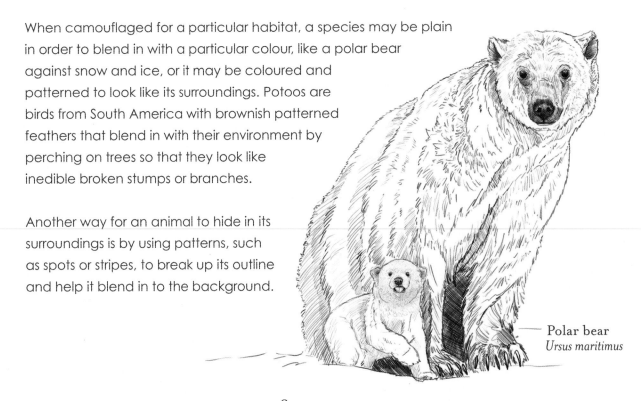

Polar bear
Ursus maritimus

The spots of leopards and cheetahs coupled with their careful movement make these big cats hard to see as they slowly stalk their prey through a maze of tangled branches, long grasses and broken shadows. This is vitally Important to both cats, because they need to get within a short distance of their prey to stand a chance of catching it.

Cheetah
Acinonyx jubatus

More complex forms of camouflage include not just colour but also pattern, shape and even behaviour. The satanic leaf-tailed gecko resembles the dead leaves it hides and hunts among not only in its colour and pattern, but also in how it holds its body. This gecko stands motionless with its body stiff and curved to resemble a dead leaf and, if it feels threatened, will even flatten itself against whatever it's standing on in order to reduce its shadow.

Let's look at some other creatures who use this skill to stay hidden.

Satanic leaf-tailed gecko
Uroplatus phantasticus

37

Chameleons

I have loved chameleons for as long I can remember. As a child, I would watch them for hours as they moved with their unique, slow, swaying steps. With eyes that can move independently of one another, long sticky tongues, strange inward-facing feet, and the ability to change colour, they seem like the work of a mad scientist.

Chameleons are a distinctive group of around 200 lizards that can be found from the southern tip of Africa all the way to India and Sri Lanka. The smallest member – the male *Brookesia micra* – measures only 1.5 centimetres long. Meanwhile, the largest – the Malagasy giant – can grow to almost 69 centimetres in length. Interestingly, both species can be found only in Madagascar, along with nearly half of all other chameleon species.

Chameleons spend the majority of their lives in the forest canopy, and their inward-facing feet are perfect for grasping twigs and branches. Their tails are also prehensile.

Brookesia micra

A chameleon's eyes can swivel through a huge range of motion completely independently of one another. This allows a chameleon to scan almost all of the surrounding area for predators or prey without moving.

A chameleon feeds mostly
on insects, which it catches with
its incredible hidden tongue, which
shoots towards its prey at speeds of up to
2.6 kilometres per second. It is also very long – up to twice
the chameleon's own body length – and coated in saliva
400 times stickier than a human's.

Perhaps the most well-known thing about chameleons is their ability to
change colour. It may seem as though they do this to hide, but their colours often
match the environment anyway. Instead, they use this skill for two key reasons:
to communicate, and to regulate their body temperature.

When it comes to communicating with one another, chameleons are highly
skilled at changing skin tone or colour as a signal to potential mates or rivals.
For example, the female common chameleon displays bright yellow spots to
show that she's ready to mate, while the male veiled chameleon uses vibrant
stripes to show off his confidence when he meets other males.

As for body temperature, chameleons are cold-blooded. Since lighter colours
are better at reflecting the sun's rays, a chameleon can make itself a lighter
colour to cool down. Likewise, deeper shades absorb heat from the sun, so
changing to a darker colour helps a chameleon to warm up.

Clouded leopard

Neofelis nebulosa

More at home in the trees than on the ground, the clouded leopard can be found from the foothills of the Himalayan mountains, across mainland Southeast Asia and into Western China. It is the smallest of the big cats, a group that also includes tigers, lions and jaguars. The clouded leopard has the longest canine teeth compared to its size of all the big cats – its canines match a tiger's in length, despite the fact that the clouded leopard is much smaller.

Shy, nocturnal and well camouflaged, the clouded leopard is named after the distinctive cloud-shaped patches on its coat. The leopard's limbs and belly are patterned with a mixture of large and small black patches, its tail is circled with thick black rings, and the back of its neck is marked with two black stripes. This combination of different shapes and colours breaks up the cat's outline, helping it to blend in to the shadows while sunlight or moonlight filters through the branches of its forest home.

Clouded leopards are extremely well adapted to life in the trees. Their short legs, wide paws and long tails – which can be the same length as their bodies – make them excellent climbers. They are even able to climb along the underside of branches using their sharp claws for grip, and can stay completely still, hanging upside down for long periods of time as they wait, hidden, for their prey.

Clouded leopards prey on a wide variety of different species, from monkeys to porcupines. They either stalk their prey or lie in wait for it before pouncing on it and killing it with a bite to the neck.

While the exact numbers of this secretive big cat are not known, they are in decline. This is due to a combination of habitat loss and poaching, and it is believed that there are fewer than 10,000 clouded leopards left.

African penguin
Spheniscus demersus

The African penguin – known in South Africa as the jackass penguin because of its loud, donkey-like bray – is my favourite of all penguins, not least because the last place that most people would expect to find a penguin is in southern Africa, thousands of miles from any snow. African penguins live in colonies on 24 islands that lie between Namibia and South Africa, and in two colonies on the mainland near Cape Town, at Boulders Beach and Betty's Bay.

I've swum alongside these characterful little birds since I was a child. While their little legs and flightless wings make them awkward on land, once in the water they transform into graceful swimmers, their wings powering them along like a bird in the sky. African penguins are fairly small, growing up to 70 centimetres tall.

Camouflage probably isn't the first thing that springs to mind when you think of a penguin's stylish, tuxedo-like pattern, but that is precisely what their black-and-white colouring is. Each penguin has a black back and white belly, with a black stripe and spots on its chest, and its pattern is as unique to it as a fingerprint is to a human. This two-toned pattern is known as 'countershading', and it might not help much on land, but in the water it helps the penguin hide. When the penguin is seen from above, its dark back blends in with the dark waters below it. Meanwhile, when it's seen from below, its light belly blends in with the sunlit waters above – and this is particularly useful when you share the water with sharks!

Although once numerous, the population of African penguins is declining rapidly, having fallen from an estimated 1.5 million birds in 1910 to less than 50,000 today. At this rate of decline, the endangered African penguin is very sadly expected to be extinct in the wild by 2026, and my heart breaks at the thought of it.

Zebras

With distinctive stripes that make them one of the most recognizable species on Earth, zebras might seem like a strange addition to this book. However, zebras are actually hidden in plain sight – and that's what makes them so interesting.

The three species of zebra are found across much of southern and eastern Africa. Plains zebra and Grévy's zebra live in a variety of different habitats, while the mountain zebra prefers steeper landscapes. Once widespread, all are now threatened, due to a mixture of hunting and habitat loss.

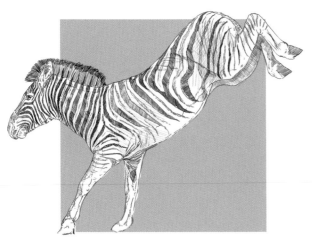

These relatives of horses and donkeys are very social, living together in groups of around fifteen individuals and often mixed with other grazing animals, such as wildebeest. Zebras have excellent eyesight and hearing. They can turn their ears in any direction independently of one another, and they take it in turns to graze while others stand guard.

When threatened, zebras run – and this is when their striped pattern really comes into its own, through a phenomenon known as 'motion dazzle'. A herd of running zebras becomes a surging, wavelike group that appears to move as one, with each animal's stripes breaking up its outline. The result is a dizzying mass of bold stripes, tossing manes and stamping hooves that looks like it's moving forward and backwards at the same time. This makes it difficult for predators to lock on to a single animal. Furthermore, some scientists believe a zebra's stripes help to keep away biting flies because the flies dislike landing on striped surfaces.

Like a human fingerprint, each zebra's pattern is unique. No one is certain why this is the case, but some have suggested that it might help individual zebras to recognize one another from a distance.

44

Plains zebra
Equus quagga

Helmeted guinea fowl
Numida meleagris

These spotted birds have a harsh and memorable call somewhere between the sound of a braying donkey and a rusty door hinge creaking. It is a sound that reminds me of my childhood, and my family even kept some guinea fowl on our little farm in England as a reminder of our time in Africa.

Helmeted guinea fowl have distinctive black-and-white spots and bald heads. They can be found all over Africa, from rolling savannahs to grassy street sides and gardens. They're one of the oldest members of a group called Galliformes (which includes turkeys, chickens and pheasants), and their fossils date back to the Eocene period, around 40 million years ago.

These guinea fowl form flocks of up to 30 birds, and travel behind herds of animals such as buffalo and wildebeest. They forage for a wide variety of foods, including seeds, insects and small lizards, as well as ticks and other pests that are disturbed by the moving herds.

The helmeted guinea fowl's characteristic call and speckled appearance gave rise to one of my favourite folktales, 'How Guinea Fowl Got Her Spots'.

In the beginning, when all was new, Guinea Fowl was a small bird with dull black feathers. She was not speckled like she is today.

Guinea Fowl was friends with Cow. They would walk together for hours, Cow munching grass and Guinea Fowl scratching in the dirt for bugs and seeds.

When Cow ate, she had her head down and couldn't see danger, so Guinea Fowl acted as her eyes. Many times, Guinea Fowl's raucous call would save Cow from hunters, such as Lion, slinking through the long grass of the savannah.

Cheated of his meal by her alarm call, Lion hated Guinea Fowl. So, to keep her friend safe, Cow dipped her tail in some milk and sprinkled Guinea Fowl with it. This gave Guinea Fowl the distinctive black-and-white pattern she has to this day, which allows her to better hide in the dappled light that shines through the long grasses of the plains.

I love this simple story because it clearly describes both the relationship between the helmeted guinea fowl and other animals, and how the pattern of a guinea fowl's feathers camouflage it by breaking up its outline.

HIDDEN FROM SIGHT

Many animals survive by keeping out of sight of predators. Some live in caves or on islands, and others stay underground.

Some creatures stay hidden by being nocturnal, which means they are mostly active at night. However, while this can help some animals to avoid predators, it can also work against them. One of the reasons that lions often prefer to hunt at night is because many of their prey have poor night vision.

Some creatures are so small that they can simply go unnoticed – and being hard to see is a good thing when everything around you wants to eat you. The fast and wary wood mouse, a tiny rodent from Europe and northwestern Africa, uses its dark fur and small size to hide at night and avoid detection by predators, such as foxes, weasels and owls.

When animals find themselves isolated from the rest of their species – on an island, for example – they frequently evolve in ways that are wildly different to how their relatives on the mainland evolve. Some move to the trees or the seas, or change their diet and appearance. Over time they may abandon some of the characteristics their close relatives exhibit. Some even become entirely new species along the way. A land-living reptile may take to the waters or a bird may keep its wings but no longer use them to fly, like the flightless cormorant from Ecuador's Galapagos Islands, which settled on the predator-free islands and eventually became flightless, since they had no enemies, and no longer needed to travel long distances to breed.

Eyelash viper
Bothriechis schlegelii

This section of the book explores a number of species that stay out of sight.

Pygmy marmoset

Cebuella pygmaea

Some creatures manage to remain hidden simply by virtue of being small. After all, it's much easier to remain unnoticed if there's not much of you to spot in the first place.

The pygmy marmoset, a species of monkey that lives in the South American rainforest, is so small as to be almost invisible. Weighing in at just over 100 grams, it is the smallest monkey in the world and one of the smallest primates – only Madame Berthe's mouse lemur from Madagascar is smaller.

Pygmy marmosets are black, grey and golden brown, and spend their lives high in the trees, living together in troops of between two and nine adults and their offspring.

This tiny primate's adaptations to tree-living include the ability to rotate its head 180 degrees, so it can look for danger, sharp, clawlike nails, which it uses to cling to branches, and a long tail for balance. Walking on all fours, it can leap up to 5 metres between trees – that's nearly 50 times its own body length.

All of these abilities come in handy should the pygmy marmoset need to make a quick escape from its predators, which include small cats, snakes such as the eyelash viper, and various raptors and birds of prey such as the harpy eagle.

Namaqua rain frog

Breviceps namaquensis

One way to stay safe is to spend most of your time under the ground, and the Namaqua rain frog is my favourite example of a creature that uses just such a strategy. This small, desert-dwelling amphibian is found in South Africa, Namibia and Zimbabwe.

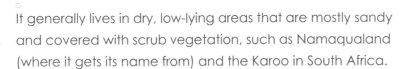

It generally lives in dry, low-lying areas that are mostly sandy and covered with scrub vegetation, such as Namaqualand (where it gets its name from) and the Karoo in South Africa.

The Namaqua rain frog's squat, round little body, short, narrow head, large eyes and thin, unhappy-looking mouth give it a permanently angry expression. It spends most of its time burrowed into the sand, where it is cool and moist, and comes out only at night to feed on insects and their larvae. When threatened, this little frog can inflate its body to significantly larger than its original size, and also squeaks in order to deter predators.

Unlike most amphibians, Namaqua rain frogs exist and breed completely out of the water. They lay their eggs in underground chambers and covered in a thick, jellylike substance. When the eggs reach the tadpole stage, this jelly softens into a fluid, which the tadpoles live in until they transform into frogs, and then set off to dig their own tunnels.

Barn owl

Tyto alba

Nocturnal creatures generally have highly developed senses of hearing and smell, and specially adapted eyesight. Many nocturnal creatures even have eyes that are large in comparison to their body size, because of the lower light levels at night. One example is the galago (also known as the bush baby), and common barn owls are another.

Along with large, specialized eyes, the barn owl also has excellent hearing, and even its heart-shaped face is an adaptation to living and hunting at night. The feathers of the owl's face form a disc, which acts like a radar dish and guides sounds into its ears. What's more, the barn owl can alter the shape of the disc at will, using special facial muscles. This allows the owl to focus on different types of sound and better pinpoint its prey.

Like most owls, the barn owl flies silently. This helps it catch the small, ground-dwelling mice and voles it hunts in its various habitats across most of the world. Barn owls also rely on their incredible ears to catch prey – not only are their ears super sensitive, they are asymmetrical, which means they are different shapes and one ear is positioned higher on the owl's head than the other. When a barn owl hears the sound of prey moving through leaves or grass, it uses its asymmetrical ears to pinpoint where the creature is. There is a tiny time difference between when the sound hits the owl's left and right ears, and this helps it to swoop down to exactly the right spot.

Many other species of owl also have asymmetrical ears, for example, the spotted eagle owl. Although this owl has 'ear tufts' that make it look as if both ears are on top of its head, it in fact has asymmetrical ears set on the sides of its head.

Spotted eagle owl
Bubo africanus

Wood mouse
Apodemus sylvaticus

Komodo dragon

Varanus komodoensis

Sometimes, when a species is isolated on a hidden island, they change size in response to their environment. For example, small animals face fewer threats and have plenty of space to get larger – and perhaps even fill a gap that, somewhere else, might be occupied by another animal. Meanwhile, large animals can face a lack of resources to sustain themselves, and so a smaller habitat means they have to become smaller to survive.

The Komodo dragon of the islands of Indonesia is one such creature. Growing up to 3 metres long, it is actually an enormous lizard and fills a role on its island home that might be occupied elsewhere by other large carnivores, such as tigers. Despite their huge size, the largest Komodo dragons only need to eat twelve times a year. Each time, they eat up to 80 per cent of their body weight, then live off the stored energy until the next time they feed.

Although mostly solitary, Komodo dragons do sometimes live and hunt in groups, actively cooperating with one another. This behaviour is unique among reptiles.

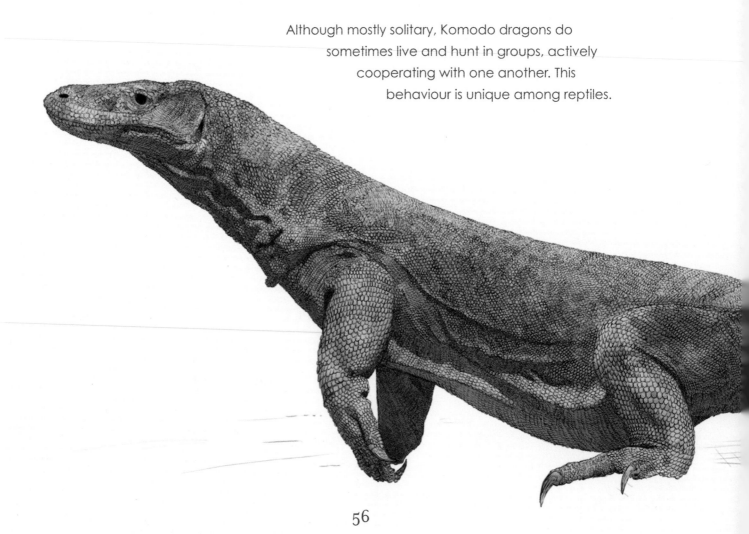

A Komodo dragon's bite is deadly. For a long time, this was thought to be because the giant lizard is a scavenger, so its mouth must be filled with lethal bacteria that would infect and kill any prey that managed to escape an initial attack. However, it has since been discovered that there are in fact two glands in the lizard's lower jaw that secrete toxic proteins, making the Komodo dragon one of only a handful of venomous lizards in the world.

Surely the Komodo dragon's most amazing adaptation is that the female can reproduce without a male, through a process called 'parthenogenesis'. Female Komodo dragons are able to produce clutches of eggs that hatch to produce only male young. The females can then create a new population by breeding with the males, and this results in both male and female young. This is a superb adaptation for surviving life in an isolated spot like an island.

Komodo dragon
Varanus komodoensis

Cave life

For a number of reasons, many creatures live in hard-to-reach places, like caves. Some nocturnal species, such as bats, use it as a way to avoid predators – after all, it's hard for something to eat you if it can't find you. These creatures roost and breed in the darkness, and sleep away the days safe in their roosts, only going outside under the cover of night to find food.

Troglobites are creatures that have adapted very well to life underground or in a cave, and they never leave. Some may be fish, spiders, beetles or millipedes that once entered a cave and became trapped and then evolved, or they may even be creatures that have always lived that way.

One thing these cave-dwellers often have in common is that they are very specially adapted to living where they do. Since troglobites cannot survive for long outside, they cannot travel between separate cave systems. As a result, many troglobites can only be found in a single cave system, which makes them particularly vulnerable to any change in their environment.

Many species are blind or completely white, as there is no need for eyes or colours when there is no light to see by or be seen by. To make up for the senses they've lost, several species have developed very good hearing, smell and touch. Many have long antennae full of sensory receptors that allow them to 'see' their world without eyes.

Cave-dwelling pseudoscorpion
Titanobochica magna

Brown long-eared bat
Plecotus auritus

The olm, a pale salamander from central and southeastern Europe, is one such example. Unlike most amphibians, which can live in or out of water for periods, the olm spends all of its life underwater. Completely blind, it uses its excellent senses of smell and hearing to find the small insects, shrimps and snails it feeds on.

When food is scarce, an olm can survive for up to ten years without food. This is due to another adaptation to cave life: a slow metabolism, which means its body processes food and nutrients much more slowly and therefore uses energy extremely efficiently. Since meals underground can be few and far between, it is very important for the creatures that live there to make them count.

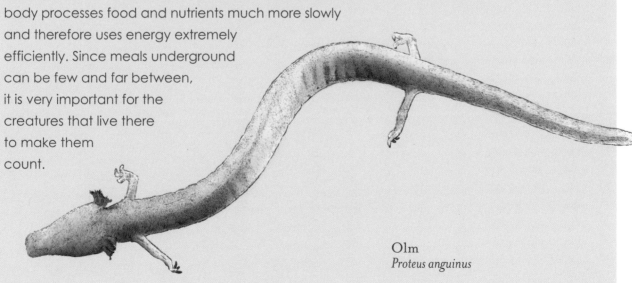

Olm
Proteus anguinus

Collared sunbird
Hedydipna collaris

CONVERGENT EVOLUTION

Ruby-topaz
hummingbird
Chrysolampis mosquitus

One of the most fascinating and sometimes hidden processes in nature is something called 'convergent evolution'. This is when organisms that are not closely related develop similar features as a result of having to adapt to the same kind of environments.

Flight is a perfect example. Birds, bats, insects and the now-extinct pterosaurs each independently evolved the ability to fly, but how they did so differs widely from species to species. These differences can be seen in the structure of the wings of each species. For instance, the wings of a bird are very different to those of a bat. A bat's wing is a membrane of skin stretched across four extremely elongated fingers and the bat's legs. Meanwhile, the flying surface of a bird's wing is made of feathers, attached to their forearm and the fused bones of what were once a wrist and hand. Only tiny fragments of two fingers remain, each anchoring a single feather.

Top: Bat wings; *Bottom:* Bird wings

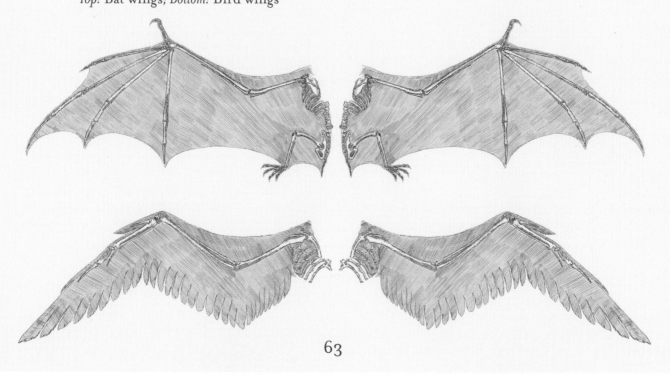

63

One of the things I find particularly interesting is how frequently creatures that are completely unrelated can come to look like one another. I've long been fascinated by birds, and especially by brightly coloured ones like the sunbird. I first saw sunbirds as a child in my grandmother's garden in South Africa, and as I watched them go from flower to flower, I noticed how similar they were to hummingbirds – both in appearance and in behaviour.

Sparkling violetear hummingbird
Colibri coruscans

Sunbirds and hummingbirds are so similar, in fact, that if you were to put certain species side by side you might think they were the same bird – or at least closely related. Both are small and fast, with brightly coloured feathers and long, curved beaks that they use to reach deep into flowers and feed on nectar. However, sunbirds and hummingbirds are not closely related at all.

Tree swallow
Tachycineta bicolor

Eurasian magpie
Pica pica

Malachite sunbird
Nectarinia famosa

Hummingbirds
are found in the
Americas, whereas
sunbirds are found across
Africa and Southeast Asia.
Not only are the two birds separated
by thousands of miles, but also by family.
Hummingbirds are actually more closely related
to swifts, and sunbirds to swallows, magpies
and crows, than they are to one another.

All of the striking similarities between the two birds actually
evolved through convergent evolution, as their environment
has led to them adapting with similar structural features.

Greater kudu
Tragelaphus strepsiceros

MALES VERSUS FEMALES: DIMORPHISM

Sometimes, males and females of the same species are very different from each other – they may differ in size, weight, colouring, markings and even behaviour. This kind of difference is called dimorphism, and it can happen for many reasons.

Differences between males and females of the same species are related to 'mate selection', which is when creatures with favourable features are more likely to reproduce and therefore adapt to their environment. For example, in some species (and in most mammals), the male is often much larger than the female. This is because the male generally performs a role that relies on strength, such as defending his family and territory from attack. He may even have extra or oversized parts like horns, tusks or antlers to help him do this, as seen in species like deer. By contrast, in many insects it is often the female that is much larger than the male, as this allows her to carry and lay more eggs.

Another reason for differences between males and females is access to food. In birds of prey, such as eagles, the female tends to be larger than the male. This is so that she can better feed herself and her chicks.

While many species use camouflage to blend in to their surroundings and avoid detection, male birds of paradise, peacocks and pheasants boast extravagant finery – and, as a result, appear to be offering themselves up as someone else's dinner! However, what they are really doing is making sure they'll get to pass on their genes, because their impressive feathers increase their chances of attracting a mate.

Indian peafowl
Pavo cristatus

The male common pheasant lives for less than a year in the wild, while the female lives for twice as long, but his ability to attract a mate doesn't depend on how long he lives – it depends on whether females will find him attractive. His brightly coloured feathers demonstrate to potential mates that he is fit, healthy and a good choice to father chicks, as an unhealthy male wouldn't be able to survive for long with such bright colours.

Over a very, very long period of time, the traits that set the males of a species apart from the females become more and more pronounced – the colours brighter, the antlers and horns larger and more impressive. Today, we see these differences in many forms, and a few of my favourite examples are explored in this section.

Common pheasant
Phasianus colchicus

Lion

Panthera leo

The lion is one of the most recognizable species in the world, and one of the largest big cats, second (only just!) to the tiger. Lions are dimorphic, with the male being much larger and heavier than the female – the male sometimes weighs up to twice as much as a lioness. With his powerful frame, deep roar and impressive mane, the male lion more than lives up to the title 'King of the Beasts'. However, despite his reputation, it is actually the lioness that does most of the work.

One unique thing about lions is that they are the only cats that live in groups. They form family units called prides, which can consist of up to three closely related males and a dozen or so lionesses and their cubs. The pride's lionesses are also related, because female cubs usually stay with the pride as they grow. Male cubs, meanwhile, eventually leave to establish their own family by taking over a pride belonging to another male.

A male lion's job is to defend his pride's territory, which can cover up to 100 square miles. He does this by scent-marking, roaring and – if necessary – chasing off intruders.

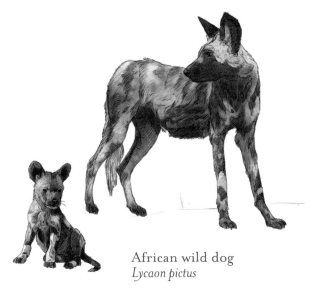

African wild dog
Lycaon pictus

Female lions, meanwhile, do most of the hunting, as well as raising the cubs. Lionesses do sometimes hunt alone, and are capable of bringing down prey twice their size. However, when they work together, lionesses are able to hunt prey that is much faster and larger than they are and would therefore be hard for one lioness to bring down on her own. Such prey includes antelopes, zebras, wildebeest and buffaloes.

In spite of their impressive hunting abilities, it turns out that lions would actually rather steal a meal from hyenas, leopards or wild dogs than catch it for themselves.

Lions are celebrated for their courage, size and strength, but they need our help. Endangered in much of their habitat, today they are found only in fragmented parts of sub-Saharan Africa, with one very small and vulnerable population of Asiatic lions in India's Gir National Park.

Cape buffalo
Syncerus caffer

Harpy eagle
Harpia harpyja

Named after the half-human, half-bird monsters of ancient Greek legends, the harpy eagle could easily be a phoenix or other mythical creature. However, this flying raptor with a giant hooked beak and claws the size of a grizzly bear's is very real – especially if you're a monkey or a sloth!

Found in the lowland, tropical rainforests of Central and South America, the harpy eagle is one of the largest and most powerful birds of prey in the world. A harpy eagle can grow up to 1 metre long and have a wingspan of around 2 metres.

Harpy eagles prey mainly on sloths and monkeys, using a variety of powerful senses to catch them. The feathers on a harpy eagle's face form a disc that focuses sound to improve the bird's hearing. They also have excellent eyesight, and are able to see something the size of a postage stamp from over 200 metres away.

Flying at speeds of up to 80 kilometres per hour on short but powerful wings, harpy eagles hunt beneath the forest canopy and pull their hapless prey from the trees. Their legs are as thick as a man's wrist and, with the longest talons of any living animal, they have some of the most powerful feet in nature. When harpy eagles attack, they are able to exert hundreds of kilograms of pressure, crushing the bones of their prey and killing it instantly.

Although male and female harpy eagles have identical plumage, the females are significantly larger than the males. Nobody is quite sure why, but one suggestion is that the female's larger size is due to her need to defend her nest against predators as she sits on her eggs before they hatch and then rears her chicks.

Ribbon-tailed astrapia
Astrapia mayeri

Birds of paradise

Birds of paradise are one of the best examples of dimorphism in nature. While the males display incredible plumage, the females have brownish feathers for camouflage. So extravagant are the males, in fact, that they appear to be an entirely different species from the females.

There are 39 different species of birds of paradise, and all are found in eastern Indonesia, Papua New Guinea and eastern Australia. Most inhabit dense rainforest and feed on fruits and insects.

As a family, birds of paradise vary as wildly from one another as they do from female to male. They range in size from the tiny 16-centimetre king bird of paradise (*Cicinnurus regius*) to the appropriately named greater bird of paradise (*Paradisaea apoda*), which is nearly three times as large.

Male birds of paradise come in every colour under the sun, including vivid blues, greens and reds, and even colours that appear to be there one moment then gone the next. Some males have head plumes, while others have chest, tail or back plumes. Others have no plumes at all. All of this astonishing variation is for one purpose only: to attract the attention of a female.

Male birds of paradise put their extraordinary feathers and dazzling colours on show in elaborate displays designed to attract a mate. The male makes strange sounds and performs a particular sequence of precise movements that females are looking for – such as bobbing his head, bouncing on the spot, and swaying and jumping from side to side.

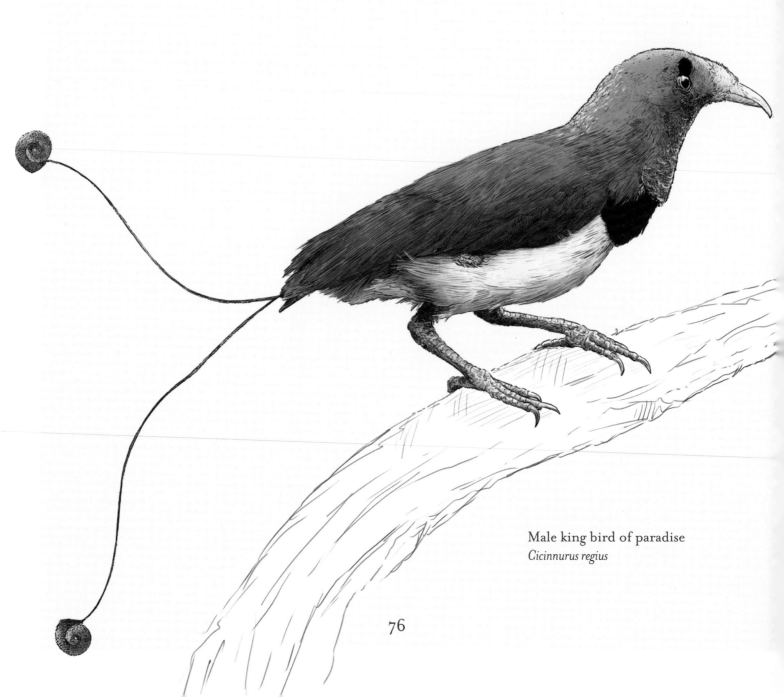

Male king bird of paradise
Cicinnurus regius

He spends hours each day practising his special dance and maintaining his performance area, carefully clearing it of dead leaves and twigs. The male then waits for a female to approach before launching into his performance, precisely positioning himself to show off his magnificent plumage to best effect.

Many of the different species of birds of paradise are endangered. This is due to them either being hunted for their colourful feathers, which are used for dresses or in various rituals, or because they are threatened by habitat destruction, mainly deforestation.

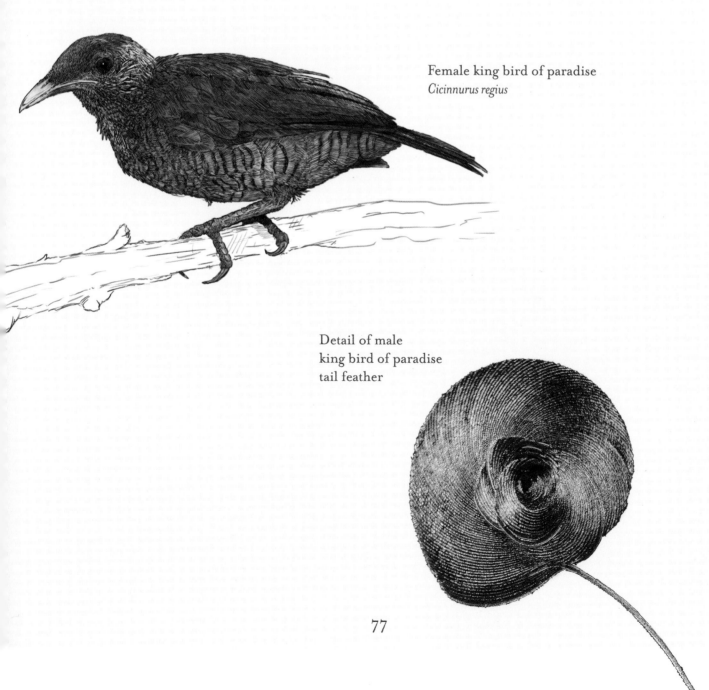

Female king bird of paradise
Cicinnurus regius

Detail of male
king bird of paradise
tail feather

77

THE SECRETS OF COLOUR

It may seem a simple feature, but an animal's colour can actually be quite complicated, with lots of hidden secrets. Animals use colour in many clever ways for many reasons, from camouflage to signalling. Some use colours to warn would-be predators that they are dangerous, while others copy the colours of more dangerous species, despite being harmless themselves.

There are a number of different ways that animals produce colour. Some species – particularly fish, reptiles and crustaceans – have chromatophores in their skin that contain pigments and can reflect light. Pigments are pieces of coloured material in the skin, eyes, hair or other body parts. They give the appearance of different colours, such as red, green or yellow.

Many birds, such as sunbirds, hummingbirds and birds of paradise, have very intense colours in their feathers that are the result of a second way they show colour, called iridescence, which shows us colours that aren't really there. Their feathers are covered with hundreds of thousands of tiny transparent scales that overlap in a diamond pattern and are arranged in several thin layers.

Magnificent riflebird
Ptiloris magnificus

78

European common cuttlefish
Sepia officinalis

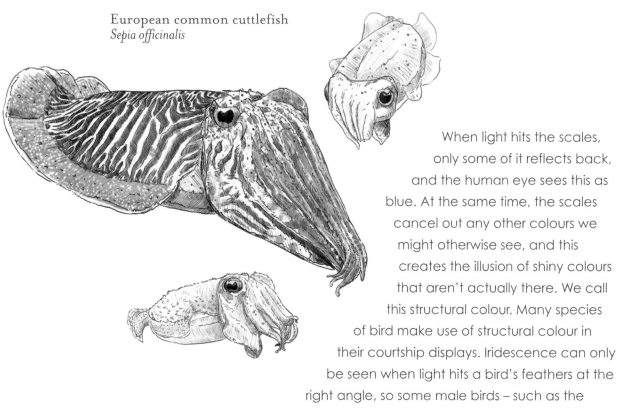

When light hits the scales, only some of it reflects back, and the human eye sees this as blue. At the same time, the scales cancel out any other colours we might otherwise see, and this creates the illusion of shiny colours that aren't actually there. We call this structural colour. Many species of bird make use of structural colour in their courtship displays. Iridescence can only be seen when light hits a bird's feathers at the right angle, so some male birds – such as the magnificent riflebird – adjust their position in relation to their audience so as to make it seem as though they can turn their colours on and off.

Some species – including cuttlefish, squid and some deep-sea fish – can produce light themselves, sometimes in different colours, and this is called bioluminescence. Other animals have specific pigments in their skin that protect against sunburn. For example, the chital deer (*Axis axis*) has a darker strip along its back, where it is most exposed to the sun. Like chameleons, some frogs are even able to lighten or darken their skin in order to help regulate their own body temperature.

There are so many amazing options when it comes to how a species might use colour. Most animals will use at least two of these things together in order to produce the various colours and effects that they need to survive.

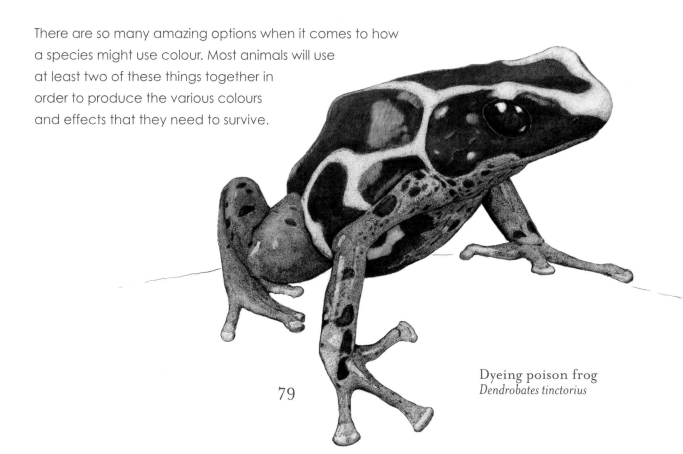

Dyeing poison frog
Dendrobates tinctorius

FEATHERS

One of the most complex and incredible structures in nature, feathers set birds apart from all other animals. Feathers evolved from the scales of reptiles, and aid birds in almost every aspect of their lives, including flying, keeping warm and dry, and communicating. Feathers even provide protection, both in a physical sense and through camouflage. The colour and shape of a bird's feathers help us to distinguish it from other bird species, and in some cases to tell the difference between males and females.

Feathers are made from keratin – the same material as human hair and nails. There are two main types of feather, known as pennaceous and plumaceous.

All feathers have the following parts:

Central shaft:
This is the hollow centre of the feather. The bottom of the shaft is smooth and extends under the skin into a space called the calamus. The top of the shaft sits above the skin, and is called the rachis. On each side of the rachis is a set of barbs. This section is known as the vane.

Barbs:
Each barb has two sets of tiny threads on it called barbules, and these cross with the ones on the barb next to it.

Barbules:
Each barbule has little hooks on it that hold the barbules together like two sides of a zip. This creates a smooth surface and maintains the shape of the feather. This strong connection holds the feather together while flying or, in the case of seabirds, swimming.

Pennaceous feathers

Flight feathers:

These are the large feathers that cover a bird's wings and tail.

Flight feathers divide further into four more categories.

- Primaries are the ten feathers at a bird's wingtip that are responsible for helping the bird move forwards while flying.

- Secondaries form the middle part of the wing and help the bird to get into and stay in the air while flying.

- Tertiaries are the feathers closest to the body.

- Tail feathers act as a brake and also help the bird to steer while flying. Most birds have ten tail feathers.

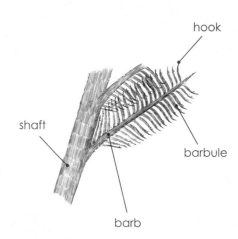

hook

shaft

barbule

barb

Contour feathers:

These feathers cover most of a bird's body. They protect the bird from the elements, and are often coloured or patterned.

contour feather

shaft

flight feathers

barbule

down feathers

barb

Plumaceous feathers

Down feathers:

These small, fluffy feathers cover the rest of the bird, sitting under the contour and flight feathers. Their job is to trap air against the bird's skin to protect it from both heat and cold.

shaft

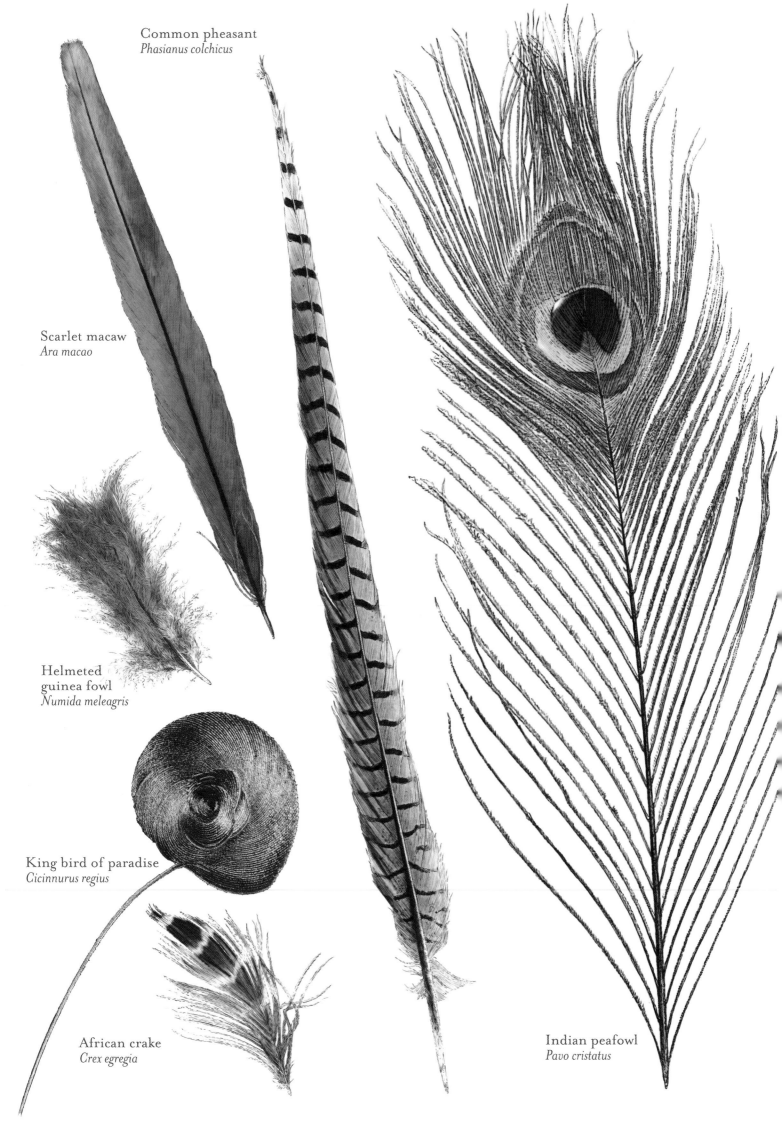

Common pheasant
Phasianus colchicus

Scarlet macaw
Ara macao

Helmeted
guinea fowl
Numida meleagris

King bird of paradise
Cicinnurus regius

African crake
Crex egregia

Indian peafowl
Pavo cristatus

Golden pheasant
Chrysolophus pictus

Helmeted guinea fowl
Numida meleagris

Rockhopper penguin
Eudyptes chrysocome

Blue jay
Cyanocitta cristata

Common ostrich
Struthio camelus

Unlike any other

Hidden in far-flung corners of our planet are rare and special species that are completely unlike any other. These species are a unique and irreplaceable part of our world. Sometimes, they represent evolutionary dead ends or they are the last of their kind. These weird and wonderful creatures are some of the most precious on our planet, but many of them are also on the verge of extinction.

Kākāpō
Strigops habroptilus

The kākāpō is a large, stocky parrot that is native to New Zealand. Kākāpō are the heaviest of all parrots, measuring up to 64 centimetres long and weighing up to 4 kilograms. With a lifespan of around 60 years, they are also the longest-living bird – some scientists even believe they may live to be 100.

Kākāpō are nocturnal, and their Māori name means 'parrot of the night'. Most parrots are brightly coloured, strong fliers and sociable, but the kākāpō is a mossy-green colour and prefers a solitary existence. The kākāpō evolved in the absence of many predators, and its wings hide the fact that it is actually flightless, running through the forest on thick, muscular legs instead.

Although the kākāpō was once widespread across New Zealand, the introduction of predators such as dogs and cats led to it becoming extinct throughout its original habitat. Now, kākāpō survive on only three small islands off New Zealand's coast, with a total population of only 147. These islands are sanctuaries and have an active conservation plan to help kākāpō to survive.

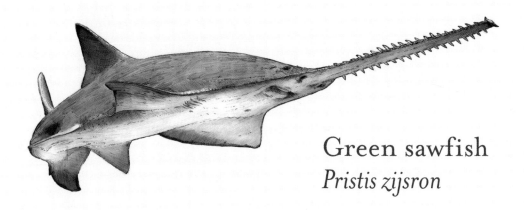

Green sawfish
Pristis zijsron

The green sawfish is the largest of all sawfishes, reaching a length of up to 7.3 metres. Its distinctive long and toothed snout (from which it gets its name) is known as a rostrum, and accounts for almost one third of the sawfish's length. The green sawfish has a lifespan of up to 50 years, and gives birth to live babies that can measure up to 80 centimetres.

A sawfish's toothed rostrum can easily become tangled in fishing nets, and as a result many sawfish end up being caught accidentally. This has led to severe population decline. Unfortunately, sawfish reproduce slowly and this means that their population is also slow to recover.

Pygmy hippopotamus
Choeropsis liberiensis

The pygmy hippopotamus is the smaller, nocturnal cousin of the more widely known common hippopotamus (*Hippopotamus amphibius*). Pygmy hippos are found in certain areas across western Africa, with the largest population in Liberia and smaller populations in Guinea, Sierra Leone and the Ivory Coast.

The name hippopotamus comes from the Greek for 'river horse', and this is a good description of the pygmy hippo, which spends much of its time hidden in rivers or swamps. Despite its resemblance to pigs and tapirs, its closest living relatives are actually whales and dolphins.

Pygmy hippos are under pressure from logging, farming, hunting and human settlement in their habitats.

Ground pangolin
Smutsia temminckii

Pangolins

The eight species of pangolin found between Africa and Asia are the only ones of their kind. These shy nocturnal animals are unique among mammals because of the large protective scales that cover their skin. Their scales are made of keratin. When startled, a pangolin will cover its head with its front legs, exposing only its scales to a potential predator. If it's touched, it will roll up into a ball and wait for the danger to go away. In fact, a pangolin's name comes from the Malay word *pengguling*, which means 'roller'.

They might look like lumbering little dinosaurs, but several species of pangolin live in trees and are excellent climbers, able to hang upside down from branches using their strong tails. They can also swim long distances and dig massive burrows up to 40 metres long.

Pangolins have very poor eyesight, and rely heavily on their senses of smell and hearing to find food and avoid danger. They also lack teeth, but this isn't a problem. They have evolved other characteristics to help them catch and eat their favourite foods, such as ants and termites. To catch its prey, the pangolin first digs into the ground, tree or vegetation using its powerful front legs and strong claws. It then uses its long tongue, which is covered in sticky saliva, to probe the inside of the insects' tunnels and retrieve its meal. Since it has no teeth, a pangolin can't chew. Instead, it swallows small stones, which sit in its stomach and help to grind up its food.

Tragically, pangolins are hugely at risk. All eight species are threatened by extinction, due to humans hunting them because their meat and scales are considered valuable in some cultures.

Hoatzin

Opisthocomus hoazin

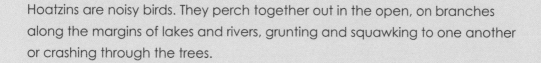

Awkward and clumsy, the hoatzin is a
bird unlike any other. This strange,
turkey-sized creature lives only in the
Amazon and the Orinoco Basin of South
America, and has no close relatives. In fact,
nobody is quite sure just what the hoatzin is related to,
but its populations are large and healthy.

Hoatzins are noisy birds. They perch together out in the open, on branches
along the margins of lakes and rivers, grunting and squawking to one another
or crashing through the trees.

A hoatzin's diet is comprised almost entirely of plants. It uses bacteria to help
digest the plant matter it consumes (like cows do), and is unique among birds
for doing so. Hoatzins are commonly known as 'stink birds', because they're
constantly fermenting leaves and are said to smell like rotting vegetation.

Hoatzins hide the fact that they can barely fly by not flying at all if they can help
it. Flying birds have strong breast muscles to help beat their wings, but hoatzins
do not. The best a hoatzin can manage is an awkward flap from one tree to
another, often landing clumsily on a nearby branch.

Hoatzins generally nest in trees that overhang the banks of rivers and lakes.
Their young are strong swimmers, and will drop into the water and swim away
to escape when threatened. Hoatzin chicks also have claws on their wings that
they use for clambering across branches and for climbing back to the nest after
taking a dip. These claws disappear as they become adults.

The strangeness doesn't stop there. A hoatzin is equally interesting to look
at, with a long, loose tuft of feathers forming a crest on the top of its head.
Its bright blue facial skin and red eyes go with its dark back, sooty-brown tail
and chestnut-coloured underparts.

HIDDEN CONNECTIONS

The natural world is made up of a dazzlingly complex series of connected ecosystems and food webs. Each and every creature in these systems – from the biggest and boldest to the smallest and seemingly least important – has a part to play. Removing any one will start a cascade of reactions that can have unexpected results.

An ecosystem is a community of living organisms together with the non-living parts of their environment, such as water and light. All of these things act together as part of an intricate mosaic.

One of the ways we understand the relationships between different organisms within an ecosystem is through food chains and food webs. A food chain shows how organisms are related to one another by the food that they eat. The first organism in a food chain is called a producer, and all the other organisms are called consumers. A producer is something like a tree, which gets energy from the sun to make its food.

A single ecosystem may contain a number of different food chains. As a result, multiple food chains can be joined together to create food webs, which better reflect the relationships between different organisms. When we look at a food web, we're able to see how seemingly unconnected creatures can be of vital importance to one another. We can also see how the removal of one organism could spell disaster for some or all of the other organisms within a particular ecosystem.

The diagram on the right shows the flow of energy around a food web – in this case, one in the African savannah. The different colours of the arrows illustrate which plants or animals are eaten by which creatures.

Cheetah
Acinonyx jubatus

Plains zebra
Equus quagga

Cape buffalo
Syncerus caffer

Grass

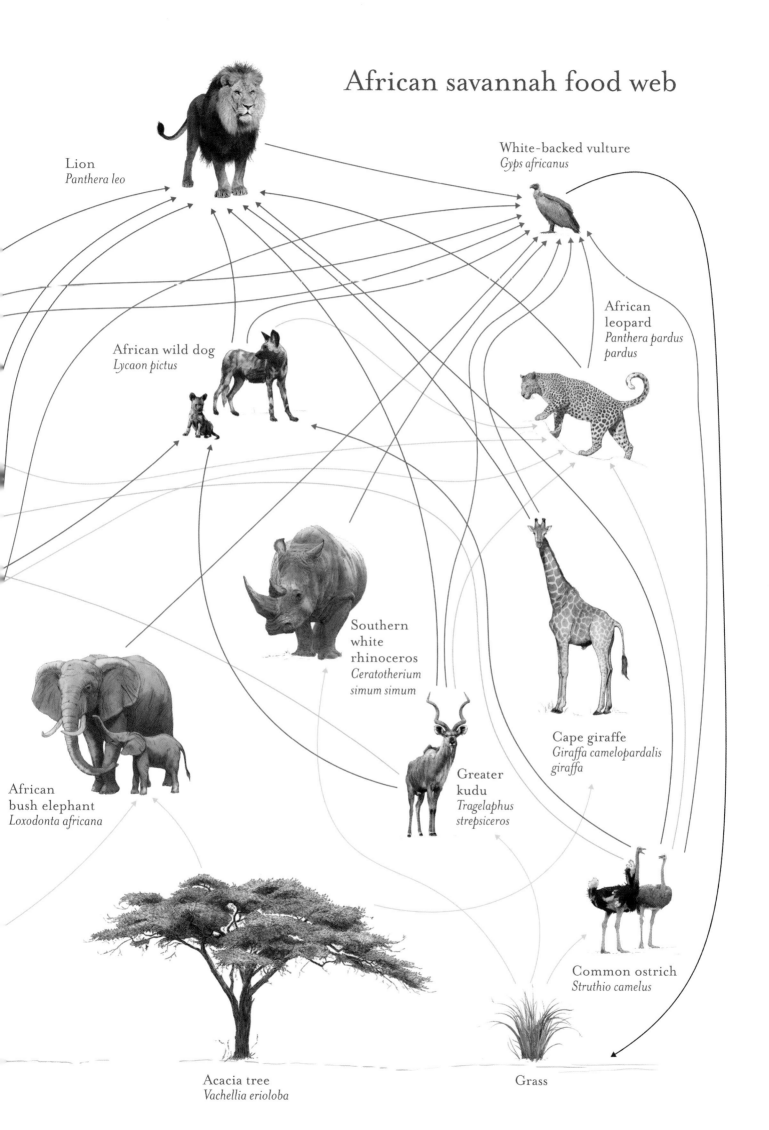

African savannah food web

Lion
Panthera leo

White-backed vulture
Gyps africanus

African leopard
Panthera pardus pardus

African wild dog
Lycaon pictus

Southern white rhinoceros
Ceratotherium simum simum

Cape giraffe
Giraffa camelopardalis giraffa

African bush elephant
Loxodonta africana

Greater kudu
Tragelaphus strepsiceros

Common ostrich
Struthio camelus

Acacia tree
Vachellia erioloba

Grass

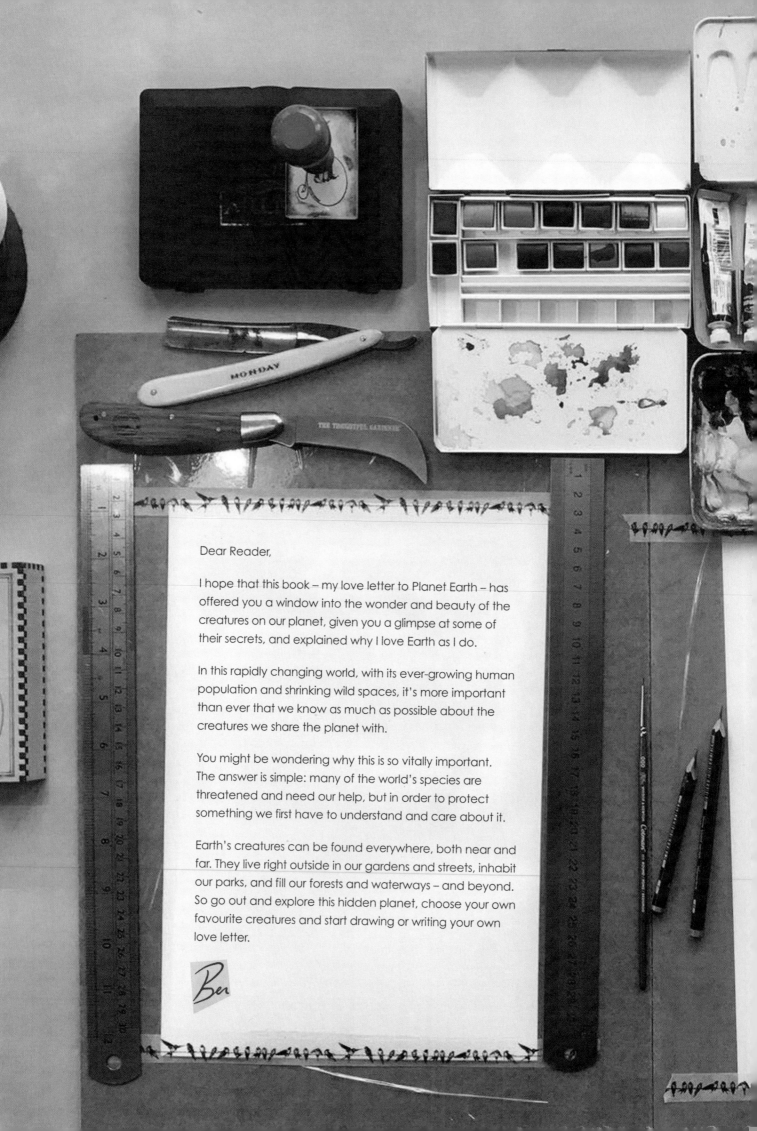

Dear Reader,

I hope that this book – my love letter to Planet Earth – has offered you a window into the wonder and beauty of the creatures on our planet, given you a glimpse at some of their secrets, and explained why I love Earth as I do.

In this rapidly changing world, with its ever-growing human population and shrinking wild spaces, it's more important than ever that we know as much as possible about the creatures we share the planet with.

You might be wondering why this is so vitally important. The answer is simple: many of the world's species are threatened and need our help, but in order to protect something we first have to understand and care about it.

Earth's creatures can be found everywhere, both near and far. They live right outside in our gardens and streets, inhabit our parks, and fill our forests and waterways – and beyond. So go out and explore this hidden planet, choose your own favourite creatures and start drawing or writing your own love letter.

Ben

INDEX

Also available

www.penguin.co.uk